MAGIC

Peter Eldin

Kingfisher

NEW YORK

KINGFISHER
Larousse Kingfisher Chambers Inc.
95 Madison Avenue
New York, New York 10016

First edition 1997
10 9 8 7 6 5 4 3 2 1

LIBRARY OF CONGRESS CATALOGING-IN-PUBLICATION DATA
Eldin, Peter.
    Magic / Peter Eldin. – 1st American ed.
        p.   cm.
    Includes index.
        1. Conjuring—History—Juvenile literature.   I. Title.
    GV1548.E36   1997
793.8—dc21   97-1424 CIP

ISBN 0-7534-5084-4

The author and publisher would like to thank Davenports and
John Fisher for their kind assistance, as well as the following artists
who contributed photographs of their acts: Blackstone Magik
Enterprises Inc; Lance Burton; David Copperfield; Tina Lenert; Slava
Polunin; Siegfried and Roy; Vik and Fabrini; Yuka.

Additional photo credits:
Bridgeman Art Library, on pages 8, 11*t* and 28*tr*; BBC Photo
Library 22*br*; The Edwin Dawes Collection 23*t* and 52*bl*; John Fisher
23*tr*; Images Colour Library / Dawes Collection 22*l*; Ivan Kyncl 25*cr*;
Peter Lane 48; Tony Stone Associates 24–25*t*; and King Features
Syndicate Inc 5*r*.

THE AUTHOR

Peter Eldin is the editor of *The Magic Circular*, the official monthly magazine of the world-famous Magic Circle, of which he is a member. Apart from a brief spell in accountancy, he has been performing and writing about magic since he left school.

THE CONSULTANT

Mike Caveney is "one of the funniest magicians in America" (*Hollywood Reporter*) and has performed all over the world, even on the Orient Express. He is a member of the exclusive Inner Magic Circle of London and a contributing editor to *Magic—The Independent Magazine for Magicians*. Mike Caveney is also a distinguished historian, lecturer, publisher, and author of books such as *Carter the Great*. He and his wife, magician Tina Lenert, live in California.

THE ILLUSTRATORS (LISTED OPPOSITE)

Simply the finest illusionists on paper. Each one conjures up their own unique interpretation of magic. Together they offer a gala performance of dazzling wit and variety. To turn the page is to dip into an inexhaustible magic box of special effects.

BEHIND THE SCENES

Editor: Camilla Hallinan, Queen of Magic
Art editor: Sue Aldworth, Sorcerer's Apprentice
Sub-editor: Rosie McCormick, Prestidigitateur of Patter
Designers: Ben White and Terry Woodley, Wonder Workers
Picture researcher: Veneta Bullen, Arch Illusionist
Cover design: Terry Woodley, Wizard Without Equal
Cover art: Paul Slater, Unassisted by Magical Apparatus
Stars and stripes: Elaine Cox, the Astral Hand
Printed in Italy

CONTENTS

(more than 50 pages of solid fun)

WORLD OF WONDERS

In the myths and legends of long ago, magicians cast evil from the land, fought dragons, created cities, and foretold the future. They also worked magic to entertain chieftains, kings, and queens. Somewhere in these tall tales, there may be a grain of truth.

▶ Perhaps the most famous magician of all was the legendary Celtic wizard Merlin. He first displayed supernatural powers when he predicted that two warring dragons (one red, one white) would be found in an underground pool beneath the castle of King Vortigern.

◄ Among the many superhuman deeds attributed to Merlin is the creation of Stonehenge. Merlin used his magic to bring massive stones from Ireland over the sea to England. Some were 13 feet tall and weighed 25 tons—they are still there, on Salisbury Plain in Wiltshire.

▼ Mandrake the Magician outwits two villainous art thieves to rescue a valuable painting.

According to legend, it was wise Merlin who trained young Arthur to become king of England 1,500 years ago. To prove Arthur was the true heir to the throne, Merlin arranged a magical test. A sword appeared, embedded in a stone—the sword was called Excalibur. He who pulled it out would be king. None but Arthur passed the test.

Comic strip heroes

Even today, long after tales of Merlin and King Arthur were first written down, there are new stories of magicians with incredible powers. Mandrake the Magician was a popular comic strip hero in the newspapers of the 1940s.

To make his escape, Mandrake borrows a horse from one painting and rides off into another!

In today's world of modern technology, conjuring tricks continue to fascinate and baffle audiences. We accept wonders such as remote control, videos and CDs, computers, the Internet, and satellite television—but we look on in amazement at the person who can make a coin vanish, produce playing cards from thin air, or restore a rope after cutting it in two. We are still intrigued by mysteries that we cannot explain.

▼ David Copperfield performs BIG magic. He has walked through the Great Wall of China and floated across the Grand Canyon. He has also made the Statue of Liberty vanish—but he did bring her back again!

Spectacular sorcery

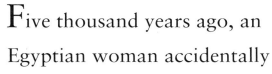

Five thousand years ago, an Egyptian woman accidentally dropped her hair ornament in a lake. A magician named Jajamanekh divided the lake in two, stacked one half on top of the other, and pulled out the ornament. Ever since, magicians have been performing some unbelievable tricks. People are apparently cut in two and then put back together, and animals appear and disappear.

▼ The magic wand has always been a symbol of a magician's power. Modern magicians do not use a wand very much and often replace it with a mystical wave of the hands.

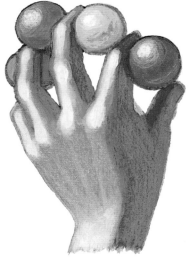

How do they do it?

Not with magic spells, but with specially built apparatus, dazzling costumes and sets, atmospheric lighting and music, dramatic gestures, and clever patter— or just a pack of cards and nimble fingers. The secret is that the magician is always one step ahead of the audience.

◄ When people think of magic they think of rabbits and top hats. But go to a magic show these days and you'll see far more spectacular costumes and tricks.

▲ Magicians have always used dramatic gestures to help bring about their magic. They make the performance seem more mysterious—and they distract the audience's attention away from what is really happening!

On a smaller scale, silk scarves change color, handcuffs unlock without a key, and one billiard ball turns into four. Large or small, these wonders are all magic and are all performed to entertain us.

MAGIC LONG AGO

No one knows who was the first magician. Perhaps it was a Stone Age cave dweller who made a pebble vanish to amuse some friends, or a stranger who rubbed two sticks together to make fire. Tales of their magic must have spread far and wide.

◄ *The Snake Charmer* was painted by **Paul Dominique Phillippoteaux** in the late 1800s. A small audience gathers in the street to watch the performance—but from a safe distance!

The first magicians of whom there is any definite proof performed for the pharaohs of Ancient Egypt. Their performances 4,500 years ago were recorded in the Westcar Papyrus, a document which is now in the State Museum in Berlin, Germany.

Weba-aner

Weba-aner is one of the magicians mentioned in the Westcar Papyrus. His special trick was to take a small wax model of a crocodile and inexplicably change it into a live, fully grown, and extremely ferocious animal!

On the road

In Europe during the Middle Ages, anyone displaying supernatural abilities might be hunted by witch-catchers, tried, and executed. Traveling magicians gave performances wherever they could before being hounded out of town. They had to travel light and their tricks were normally simple sleight of hand, performed with nimble fingers and coins or balls. Medieval clothes had no pockets, so magicians carried the tools of their trade in a bag hanging from a belt.

Magic in the market

Throughout the Middle Ages, performers such as roving minstrels, jugglers, fire-eaters, waterspouters, and stoneswallowers entertained the crowds at local markets and fairs with their skills. Those who performed sleight-of-hand tricks (by the skillful movement of their fingers) were also called jugglers.

Magicians merely pretended to change one thing into another, but alchemists hoped to do just that. Both used the latest developments in science in their shows and experiments. Ignorance about their methods brought charges of witchcraft.

► *The Alchymist* **by Joseph Wright (1734–1797) shows Hennig Brand, a German alchemist, in his laboratory**.

Alchemy

Alchemists in the Middle Ages searched for ways to turn base metals, such as iron, into gold and to build machines that, once started, would work forever without power.

Accused of witchcraft

During the 1400s in Cologne, Germany, a girl was tried for witchcraft because she tore a handkerchief to pieces and then restored it by sleight of hand—a trick still performed today. Those found guilty of witchcraft were burned at the stake, hanged, or drowned. Not until the 1700s did people realize that magicians were nothing more than skillful entertainers.

◄ **The Cups and Balls is one of the oldest tricks of all. It normally involves three cups and balls— the balls seem to move from one cup to another, or disappear from the table and reappear inside the magician's hat.**

Isaac Fawkes

One of the first to make magic respectable was Isaac Fawkes (*c.* 1675–1731). He performed not on street corners but in booths at county fairs, in private homes, and in theaters. His famous Egg Bag trick was described in an advertisement in 1726:

"He takes an empty bag, lays it on the Table and turns it several times inside out, then commands 100 Eggs out of it and several showers of real Gold and Silver, then the Bag beginning to swell several sorts of wild fowl run out of it upon the Table."

Magic comes in from the cold

During the 1700s, magic shook off any charges of witchcraft. Performances took place in drawing rooms, theaters, and palaces—and the tricks became more spectacular. Chandeliers lit the plushly carpeted stage, and tables were covered with glittering cloths. The performers were often dressed in the finest clothes, and claimed that their apparatus was solid silver or gold.

Professor Pinetti

One of greatest magicians of the late 1700s was Italian-born Giuseppe Pinetti (c. 1750–1800). Originally a professor, he began his career as a magician by entertaining his physics students. He went on to entertain the kings of Europe, and became famous for his breathtakingly lavish stage settings. One of his most celebrated tricks was firing a nail from his pistol to pin a particular card to the wall. This took several attempts to get right!

Technical wizardry

Performing in theaters gave magicians the chance to use new special effects and develop their craft. The French magician Philippe (1802–1878) featured a literally dazzling opening trick. The audience sat in total darkness until Philippe fired a pistol that lit, in an instant, 250 candles on stage. To the majority of the audience who knew nothing about the recently invented electricity, this was truly amazing.

Blitz's bullet

Audiences gasped in horror when Antonio Blitz (1810–1877) told his marksman to shoot at him. Blitz clasped his hand to his heart and staggered back. Lifting his hand, he revealed not blood but the bullet he had caught.

The Wizard of the North

As the young son of poor Scottish farmers, John Henry Anderson (1814–1874) once saw Blitz perform. From then on, he made up his mind to learn the craft of magic, and launched his own career as The Wizard of the North. Anderson became an international success. He mesmerized audiences everywhere, including Czar Nicholas I of Russia and Queen Victoria, by producing flowers from his fingertips, white doves from a magic cauldron, and bowls of goldfish from empty scarves.

We are amused

Queen Victoria's favorite trick, performed by Anderson at Balmoral Castle in Scotland, was his ability to produce birds, flowers, and even his son, from the pages of The Inexhaustible Scrapbook.

Many magicians attracted audiences by advertising their shows. As the demand for magic shows grew among the middle classes, performers were able to charge entrance fees. Some performers became so rich and successful that they opened their own theaters. Magic had finally become a respectable form of entertainment.

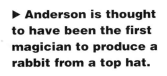

▶ Anderson is thought to have been the first magician to produce a rabbit from a top hat.

The Father of Modern Magic

 The French magician Jean Robert-Houdin (1805–1871) began his working life as a watchmaker. He did not become a magician until he was 40, when a bookseller accidentally sent him some books about conjuring. After staying up all night to read them, Robert-Houdin knew he had found what would be the great passion of his life.

Stage fright

Robert-Houdin's first professional performance was at the Palais Royal in Paris on July 3, 1845. He performed his magic tricks well, but he suffered from stage fright and the show ended in a shambles. Only Robert-Houdin's conviction that he was destined to be a great magician, and his determination to do better, got him back on stage the following evening. Soon people were flocking to see him.

Robert-Houdin is now revered as the Father of Modern Magic. He did away with the old flowing robes and dubious drapes, and brought the craft of magic to new heights.

Mechanical genius

Robert-Houdin was a master illusionist and a creative conjurer. Thanks to his training as a watchmaker, he had an amazing ability to make ingenious mechanical devices, known as automata. One of the most famous automata was The Orange Tree. First the tree blossomed and bore fruit, then butterflies pulled a handkerchief out of an orange and gently hovered above the tree. Audiences were astounded.

Second sight

One of the most popular parts of Robert-Houdin's show included his son, Emile. The boy was described by his father as having mystical powers. Although blindfolded, Emile could describe any object held up by members of the audience. (In fact, both father and son had memorized an elaborate system of code words.)

In 1856 Robert-Houdin came out of retirement on a special assignment for the French government. His task was to convince Algerian rebels that French magic was more powerful than theirs. On October 28, Robert-Houdin performed before Algerian chiefs and French military staff. He invited a tribesman to lift a wooden box—which he did without difficulty. Then he told the man he would rob him of his strength—sure enough, the tribesman was unable to lift the box again. The rebels never knew the box contained an iron plate controlled by an electromagnet under the stage.

Lighter than air

Robert-Houdin claimed that the newly developed gas, ether, could make a person float like a balloon. To demonstrate this, he levitated his son, Eugene. The audience smelled the ether burning and saw the boy float horizontally from a single cane. Was it the ether?

Panorama of posters

 During the 1800s, magic became hugely popular. Having journeyed from ancient temples to country fairs and private drawing rooms, magicians finally found a more permanent home in the great theaters of the day. To encourage a growing public interest in their craft, and promote their own careers, magicians turned to the power of advertising.

Poster power

The principal form of advertising was the poster. Beautiful and evocative art was used to lure the paying public to the theater. Some posters hinted at the strange and mysterious powers of magic. Others portrayed the magician in a striking pose, or showed one of the magician's most spectacular tricks.

An art form

The golden age of the magic poster was 1875 to 1925. One of its finest artists was French-born Jules Chéret (c. 1836–1933). His posters were always eye-catching, even when they used only three basic colors: red, green, and black.

Stock posters

Magicians who couldn't afford their own posters used stock posters instead. These were already designed and printed. The magician's name was added to a blank space on the poster. The place and date of the performance were printed separately and pasted at the bottom.

◄ **Billposters waged war on one another! They fought for the most eye-catching sites and plastered their posters on top of other people's.**

England's Home of Mystery

On May 26, 1873, two relatively unknown magicians, John Nevil Maskelyne and his partner George Cooke, appeared at a London venue known as Egyptian Hall. Their performance was so inventive and original that they were an instant success. For more than 30 years they appeared regularly at Egyptian Hall and invited some of the world's greatest magicians to join them. Maskelyne also organized traveling shows to reach people who couldn't come to London. By the end of the 1800s, Egyptian Hall had become the center of magic in England and gained the title, Home of Mystery.

Turned away

Maskelyne and Cooke actively encouraged new talent, but even they occasionally got it wrong. They turned down a young magician who asked to appear in their show. His name was Harry Houdini.

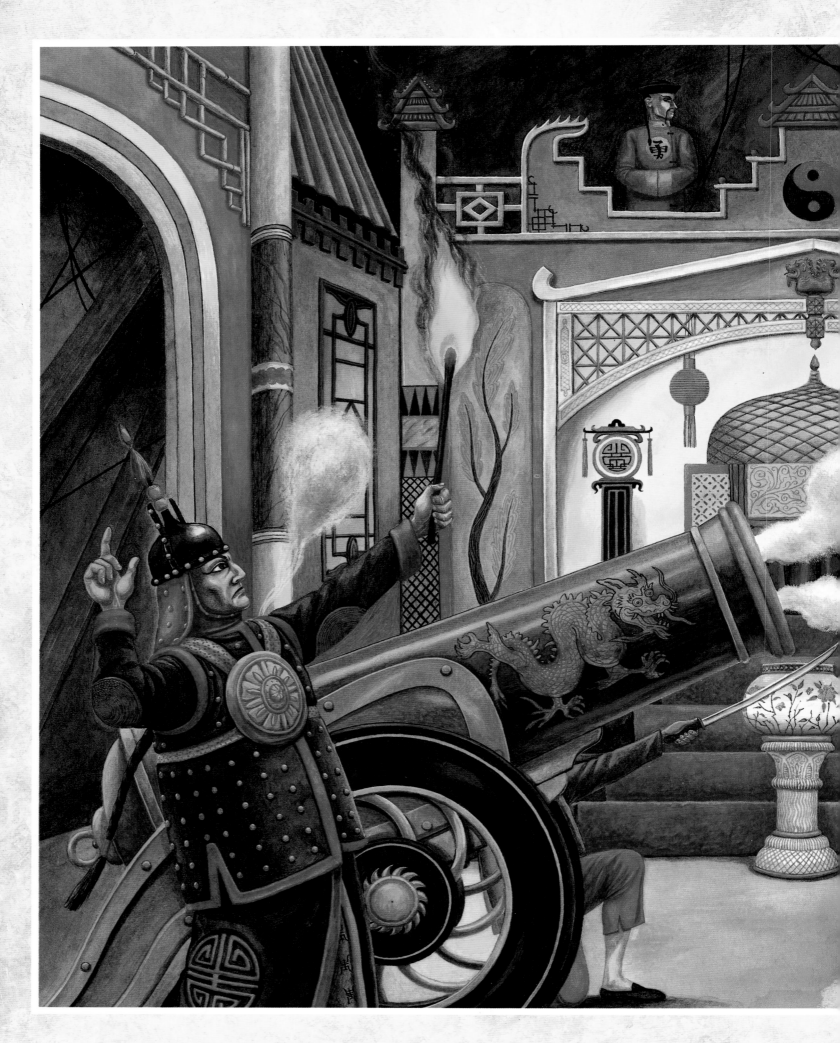

Chung Ling Soo

Born not in China but in New York on April 2, 1861, Chung Ling Soo's real name was William Ellsworth Robinson. He modeled himself on an authentic Chinese performer called Ching Ling Foo, as Eastern magic was in great demand at the time. Throughout his career, Chung Ling Soo was careful to conceal his real identity.

Cannon fire

Appearing at the London Hippodrome in 1905, Chung Ling Soo's new show surpassed anything he had done before. Breathless audiences watched as Chung Ling Soo's wife, Suee Seen, was lowered into the barrel of a cannon. The cannon was fired toward a large trunk at the back of the theater. When the trunk was opened, out stepped Suee Seen.

MODERN MARVELS

By the start of the 1900s, popular magicians were crisscrossing the globe. They took with them hundreds of crates full of stage sets and equipment, dozens of animals, from tiny birds to enormous elephants, and armies of stage hands. A new age of magic had begun.

The greatest show of all

Early in the 1900s, American magician Howard Thurston (1869–1936) toured the world with elaborate illusion shows. His *Wonder Show of the Universe* contained no less than 18 large-scale illusions. As a young boy, Thurston had run away from home to seek fame and fortune. For almost 30 years, he was America's top performer.

Magicians strove to outshine one another by creating their own highly complex illusions. Their lavishly staged shows were more challenging and more costly to produce than ever before. With the outbreak of World War II in 1939, the more extravagant shows disappeared. Money to stage them, and attend them, was hard to come by.

Houdini was born Ehrich Weiss, in Hungary. When he was four years old, his parents emigrated to the United States. A traveling circus came to town—calling himself Ehrich, Prince of the Air, he entertained the neighbors by performing on a home-made trapeze in a friend's backyard. When Ehrich was 12, he ran away from home. He wanted to be a great magician, like Robert-Houdin. So he changed his name to Houdini and began performing in small traveling shows.

No jail could hold him

Harry Houdini (1874–1926) and his feats of escapology are legendary. Challenging policemen and jailers wherever he went, he was always able to free himself from their handcuffs and cells. He even escaped from the belly of a whale and a giant laced-up football! Houdini was also a first-class illusionist. On stage he could walk through a solid brick wall or make an elephant vanish. He was the most dramatic entertainer in the world.

Get out of that!

Success escaped Houdini until, traveling to Britain, he released himself from handcuffs at Scotland Yard. This much-publicized stunt led to his first London performance at the Alhambra Theatre in 1900.

Jail break

In 1906 Houdini escaped from a prison cell in Washington, D.C. On top of that, he opened other cell doors and moved the prisoners around—much to the embarrassment of the authorities.

The showman

Houdini often performed outdoors. He knew this added a sense of drama and danger to his act. It also got great publicity. For example, his escape from a straitjacket while hanging high above the street thrilled people all over the world. When he was free, though still upside down, he bowed to the huge crowds below.

Under water

For his Chinese Water Torture act, Houdini was shackled and lowered head-first into a tank of water, which was then padlocked. Assistants stood by with axes in case things went wrong. But within two minutes Houdini was out.

Making movies

In 1918, at the height of his fame, Houdini was asked to appear in his first Hollywood movie, *The Master Mystery*. Setting up a movie company in 1920 allowed him to write and star in his own movies, such as *The Man From Beyond*, the story of a man imprisoned in ice for 100 years. In every movie, Houdini was trussed up by the villains in some spectacular way. And in every movie he managed to work his way free.

Airborne

The Wright brothers made the first airplane flight in 1903. Aviation fascinated Houdini and he bought his own plane. In 1910, at Digger's Rest near Melbourne, he became the first man to fly in Australia.

End of an era

A student had heard that Houdini could withstand a powerful blow to his stomach—but punched him before he was ready. Houdini was in agony. A few days later, on Halloween, 1926, he died.

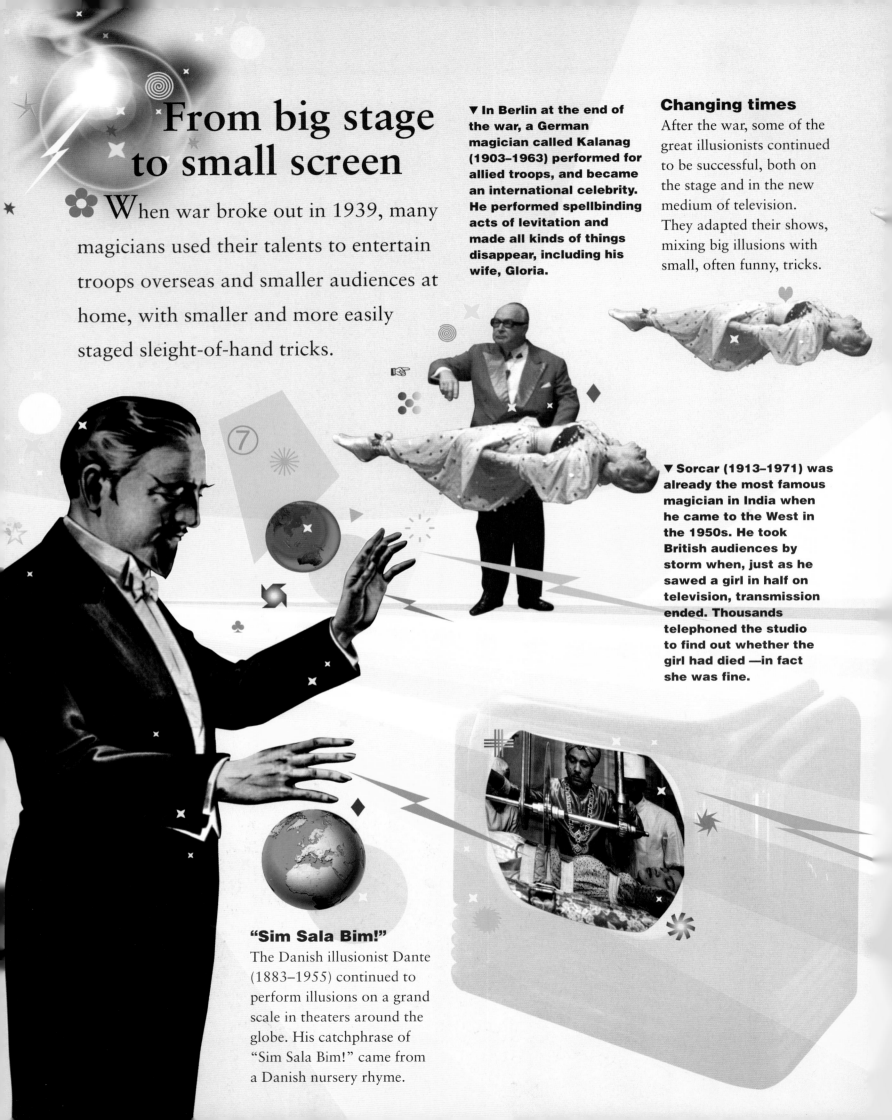

From big stage to small screen

❀ When war broke out in 1939, many magicians used their talents to entertain troops overseas and smaller audiences at home, with smaller and more easily staged sleight-of-hand tricks.

▼ In Berlin at the end of the war, a German magician called Kalanag (1903–1963) performed for allied troops, and became an international celebrity. He performed spellbinding acts of levitation and made all kinds of things disappear, including his wife, Gloria.

Changing times

After the war, some of the great illusionists continued to be successful, both on the stage and in the new medium of television. They adapted their shows, mixing big illusions with small, often funny, tricks.

▼ Sorcar (1913–1971) was already the most famous magician in India when he came to the West in the 1950s. He took British audiences by storm when, just as he sawed a girl in half on television, transmission ended. Thousands telephoned the studio to find out whether the girl had died —in fact she was fine.

"Sim Sala Bim!"

The Danish illusionist Dante (1883–1955) continued to perform illusions on a grand scale in theaters around the globe. His catchphrase of "Sim Sala Bim!" came from a Danish nursery rhyme.

The superman of magic

From the 1930s to the 1950s, Harry Blackstone, Sr. (1885–1965) was the top magician in the United States. He performed big illusions, but one small trick always stole the show. A handkerchief borrowed from the audience came alive. It wriggled out of the magician's grip, danced in and out of boxes, and flew across the stage. Finally it was caught and handed back to its owner. Blackstone was so popular that he became a comic strip hero.

After the war, audiences continued to watch magic, but few wanted to pay for a night out at the theater. Instead they stayed at home, in their armchairs, and watched magicians on television. TV cameras zoomed in closer, so some of the tricks got smaller—and more clever, too.

► Harry Blackstone, Sr.

Changing styles

In the 1960s, audiences loved the elegant dove productions of acts like Les Septembres. Turn the page and you'll see that, thirty years on, magic looks a little different.

▼ Two chimps and millions of Britons have watched Paul Daniels (b. 1938) since his first television appearance in 1970. Not even TV. close-ups reveal how he does his Chop Cup.

▼ In Vik and Fabrini's clever double act for the 1990s, an inflatable dummy seems to have a mind of its own. The two Brazilians combine mime, comedy, and magic to entertain audiences all over the world.

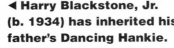

◄ Harry Blackstone, Jr. (b. 1934) has inherited his father's Dancing Hankie.

Return of the spectacular

Thanks to the reviving powers of television, the full-size magic spectacular is making an electrifying comeback. Simple sleight of hand is transformed by *Star Wars* technology in lavish shows around the globe. Las Vegas is currently the magic capital of the world, with more shows for more people than ever before.

Fan–tastic

Yuka Shimada mixes traditional Japanese dance and costume with ultra-modern jazz-fusion and a single spotlight as she produces beautiful fans and multicolored silks from thin air.

Yuka lives and breathes magic. She joined her first magic club as a college student, spent her honeymoon at a magic convention in Hawaii, won first prize in the 1984 SAM competition, and performed at Hollywood's Magic Castle—all by the age of 22.

Young master

In 1982 Lance Burton (b. 1960) became one of the youngest magicians, and the first American, to win the Grand Prix of Magic in Lausanne, Switzerland. He is now at the top of his profession, with a ten-year, hundred-million-dollar contract to perform live at the Monte Carlo Hotel in Las Vegas.

At the heart of Lance Burton's international success are his lovely dove productions. These were inspired by Channing Pollock's elegant act a generation before.

Different styles

The German illusionists Siegfried and Roy are one of Las Vegas's biggest attractions. Their show includes lions, tigers, crocodiles, flamingos, a black panther, a leopard, and other exotic animals—not to mention the metal monster you can see here.

In contrast to Siegfried and Roy on their crowded stage, the Russian clown Slava Polunin (b. 1950) stands completely alone as he performs. Audiences love the strangely beautiful mime and magic of his *Snowshow*.

Modern mystery

Without a doubt, David Copperfield (b. 1956) is the most famous magician in the world. His illusions are BIG—such as making a seven-ton Lear jet disappear!

The question is, how? People who watch magic on TV often wonder whether what they see is achieved by the magicians themselves or by the cameras. But people who have seen Copperfield live on stage realize that his magic is even more impressive than they originally thought.

▶ **Fairytale charm and clever mime are the hallmarks of a performance by Venezuelan-born Tina Lenert (b. 1948). She plays a cleaning lady who, like Cinderella, is wooed by a mysterious "prince"—but this prince is just her broom, coat, and hat.**

Live on stage and broadcast on television, magic now reaches a global audience that Houdini and Chung Ling Soo could only have dreamed of.

THE BOY

A VERY SPECIAL ROPE

THE MAGICIAN'S BASKET

THE ORIENTAL BRAZIER

CLASSICS OF MAGIC

Rings link and unlink, balls appear and disappear beneath three cups, a person is sawn in two without harm. These illusions are regarded by magicians as classics.

Often a classic is based on one simple idea, an idea that fascinates one generation after another. The classics are as popular today as they were when first performed.

◄ **Many of the great illusionists, such as Howard Thurston, Blackstone, Sr., Kalanag, Sorcar and Paul Daniels, have presented stage versions of the classic Indian Rope Trick.**

HOW IS IT DONE?

Fact or fiction?
The Indian Rope Trick is perhaps the most famous of the classics. A rope is thrown into the air, and somehow stays there. Not only that, but a child climbs up it till out of sight! Trouble is, no one in living memory has seen a genuine outdoor performance, and no one has ever claimed the rewards offered for one.

An Eastern mystery
The first eyewitness account of the Rope Trick came from a traveler, Ibn Batuta, in 1355. He saw a Chinese conjurer toss up a ball with a long strip of leather. A boy climbed up the strip and out of sight. The conjurer climbed after him, chopped him up, and threw down the pieces. Then he came down and put the boy together again.

The Juggler

Many artists have shown The Cups and Balls trick, but the best-known painting is by the 15th-century Flemish artist Hieronymus Bosch. One spectator is so entranced by the magician's performance that a thief is able to steal his purse without being noticed!

◀ Japanese magicians used very shallow cups. The balls were made from silk.

▲ In Turkey, cups were conical in shape and balls were made from cork.

◀ In India, magicians used cups with knobs on top. The balls were simply pieces of cloth filled with cotton.

Cups and balls

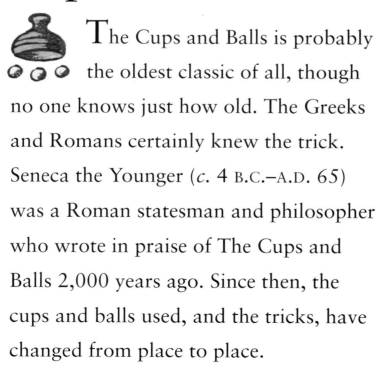

The Cups and Balls is probably the oldest classic of all, though no one knows just how old. The Greeks and Romans certainly knew the trick. Seneca the Younger (*c.* 4 B.C.–A.D. 65) was a Roman statesman and philosopher who wrote in praise of The Cups and Balls 2,000 years ago. Since then, the cups and balls used, and the tricks, have changed from place to place.

Magicians today use shiny metallic cups, and cloth-covered balls of cork.

◄ **At racetracks and fairgrounds, the trick was performed with walnut shells and peas.**

Roman magic

Roman conjurers were called *acetabularii*, after the Latin word for vinegar jar, *acetabulum*. They used an empty jar in their Cups and Balls.

▲ **Galli galli men were Egyptian magicians who often ended The Cups and Balls with chicks instead of balls.**

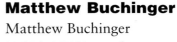

Matthew Buchinger

Matthew Buchinger (1674–1740) was known as The Little Man of Nuremburg because he was only 29 inches tall. He had no hands or legs, yet he was an expert magician. One of his favorite tricks was The Cups and Balls.

Every magician has their own favorite routine for The Cups and Balls. This variety, and the simplicity of the basic idea, explain why the trick has been so popular for so long.

The trick starts with three balls under three cups. The balls move from one cup to another. When the cups are stacked up, a ball passes right through them. In the end, there might be just one, much bigger ball—or an orange! (Some performers do the trick with only one cup—the Chop Cup.)

Hey presto!

A rabbit from an empty hat, doves from silk scarves, cards from thin air, an egg from behind your ear—for thousands of years, conjurers have been producing all kinds of objects from all kinds of places. Who knows where it will stop—the magician's imagination is limitless.

▲ Signor Antonio Blitz (1810–1877) amused guests when he began producing fruit and vegetables from a man's coat, much to the man's surprise.

◄ Cardini (1895–1973) acted the part of a tipsy man teetering across the stage. The sudden appearance and disappearance of cards or billiard balls so startled him that his monocle fell out.

◄ Producing a shower of coins from nowhere is known as The Miser's Dream. This name was invented by Thomas Nelson Downs (1867–1938), who was known as The King of Koins. He was one of the highest paid acts in the U.S.

Magicians also love to make things vanish—anything, anywhere, from a quarter in their palm to a two-ton elephant in an open field.

▼ In the 1960s a suave American performer achieved worldwide fame for his breathtaking dove productions. His name was Channing Pollock (b. 1926). He became the top magician of his day.

◄ In 1863, Blitz performed tricks for President Abraham Lincoln. While Abe's son, Tad, gasped in astonishment, Blitz pulled an egg out of his mouth.

Vanishing ladies

When Buatier de Kolta (1847–1903) draped a cloth over a woman and then whisked it away, she completely vanished. Howard Thurston (1869–1936) brought a car full of lovely ladies on stage—a puff of smoke and they were gone. David Copperfield once vanished the Statue of Liberty.

◄ Pulling a rabbit out of a top hat is supposed to be a classic. In fact, it isn't performed very much and never has been. The first person to do this trick was probably John Henry Anderson, in the 1830s.

Rings and things

 To knot and unknot, cut and uncut, link and unlink, is a recurring theme in magic. Tricks with scarves, bits of rope, and metal rings are old but still popular classics. One of the oldest is The Cut and Restored Rope—there are literally hundreds of different routines for this.

That's knot possible!

One of the specialties of the Italian-born performer Slydini (1901–1991) was to give two of his handkerchiefs to a spectator and ask her to tie them together. No matter how hard the knots were tied, they always melted apart in Slydini's hands.

Any old rope?

In The Professor's Nightmare (or Equal, Unequal Ropes) there are three ropes of different lengths—one short, one medium, and one long. They are deftly looped together, pulled apart, and shown to the audience—all three are now the same length. They end up as just one long rope!

W here would magicians be without their handkerchiefs and scarves? Called "silks" in the trade, streams of them can be produced from empty pockets and boxes, made to change color, or turned into other things completely.

▲ **Chinese Linking Rings**

Cut & Restored Rope

1

2

3

4

5

Sympathetic Silks

1

2

3

4

5

6

▶ **The Chinese Linking Rings trick really did originate in China. Although it must be very old, it was not performed by Western magicians until the 1800s. Joseph Jacobs, a British magician, launched it as part of his act in around 1835.**

First, take a pair of scissors...

The Cut and Restored Rope is one of the classics of magic. In its simplest version, a piece of rope is cut into two pieces, looped this way and that, and then magically restored. In more complicated versions the rope may be cut several times, yet all the pieces mysteriously rejoin into one long piece.

Sympathetic silks

Three silks are tied together and placed on one side of the stage. Three loose silks are put down on the other side of the stage. The magician counts them and puts them back. But the first three silks are loose—the knots seem to have moved to the other three, which are now tied together. When all six are thrown into the air they land knotted together.

In many versions of Chinese Linking Rings, the magician has eight solid metal rings. The audience can see that the rings are separate. Yet somehow they link and unlink at the magician's command. For the grand finale, they are thrown into the air to form one long chain.

Sawing through a woman

One of the tricks performed in the Middle Ages was a decapitation, known as The Decollation of John the Baptist. It would not fool audiences today, but magicians are still "chopping" people up—using more clever methods.

In 1921 a British magician, P. T. Selbit (1881–1938), caused a sensation when he sawed a woman in half. The woman was tied up in a long wooden box, and the box was sawn in two. The woman stepped out...

...without so much as a scratch!

◄ A few months after P. T. Selbit sawed through a woman in England, Horace Goldin (1873–1939) staged his rival version in New York. This time, the woman's head and feet poked out of the box and the box was pulled apart. Meanwhile an ambulance waited outside the theater with a sign saying "in case the saw slips." The saw never slipped, and the woman always survived.

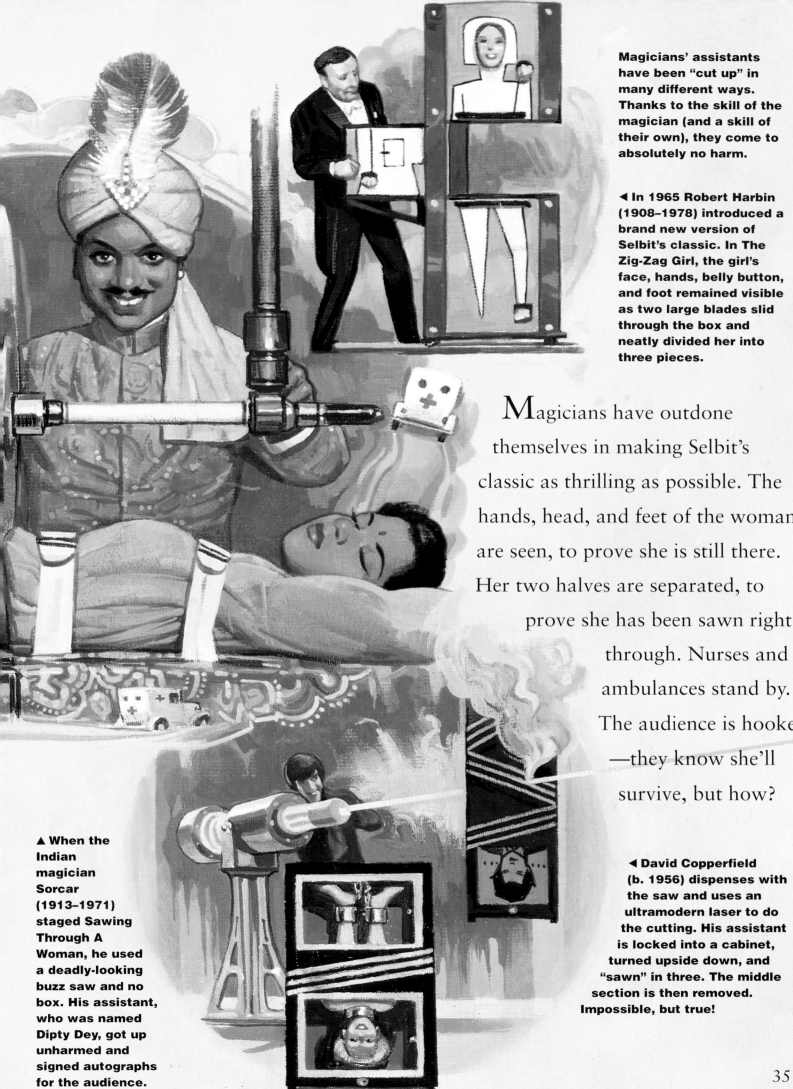

Magicians' assistants have been "cut up" in many different ways. Thanks to the skill of the magician (and a skill of their own), they come to absolutely no harm.

◀ In 1965 Robert Harbin (1908–1978) introduced a brand new version of Selbit's classic. In The Zig-Zag Girl, the girl's face, hands, belly button, and foot remained visible as two large blades slid through the box and neatly divided her into three pieces.

Magicians have outdone themselves in making Selbit's classic as thrilling as possible. The hands, head, and feet of the woman are seen, to prove she is still there. Her two halves are separated, to prove she has been sawn right through. Nurses and ambulances stand by. The audience is hooked —they know she'll survive, but how?

▲ When the Indian magician Sorcar (1913–1971) staged Sawing Through A Woman, he used a deadly-looking buzz saw and no box. His assistant, who was named Dipty Dey, got up unharmed and signed autographs for the audience.

◀ David Copperfield (b. 1956) dispenses with the saw and uses an ultramodern laser to do the cutting. His assistant is locked into a cabinet, turned upside down, and "sawn" in three. The middle section is then removed. Impossible, but true!

Up in the air

One of the most sensational illusions in the whole of magic is to defy the law of gravity by levitating something so that it rises above the ground, or suspending it so that it hovers in midair.

When Robert-Houdin performed his Ethereal Suspension in 1847, his son floated horizontally with just one elbow resting on a rod. The first person to perform a full levitation, with no visible support, was John Nevil Maskelyne at the Crystal Palace, London, in 1867. The person he levitated was his wife.

Self levitation

Early in the 1800s, Western magicians began to hear about Indian magicians who could levitate themselves. In 1876, Maskelyne had a try. Although he was first tied up in a cabinet, he floated out and up to the ceiling of the theater. He hovered above the heads of his astonished audience for a while, then floated back down to the cabinet.

Maskelyne's son, Nevil, later introduced a large hoop to pass over the woman and convince the audience that there were no attachments involved. The new genre soon caught on. Today, David Copperfield floats all around the stage. He even allows a member of the audience the thrill of "flying" with him.

Need a lift?

Henry Roltair (1853–1910) performed a levitation on himself toward the end of the 1800s. He rode around the stage on a bicycle that gradually rose into the air and looped the loop. Not content with that, Roltair later levitated a motorcar and its driver. People still wonder how he got it to float above the stage, but there's an old photograph to prove that he did!

Up, up, and away

Servais Le Roy (1865–1953) first hypnotized his wife Talma, then laid her on a couch and covered her with a sheet. As she rose into the air, Le Roy passed a hoop over her. When the sheet was whisked away, she'd gone!

The Floating Lady

One 1950s' masterpiece began as a suspension and ended as a levitation. Kalanag's wife, Gloria, lay on a board placed on two chairs. He removed the chairs and board, leaving her suspended in midair. She then rose high above his head, returned, and bowed.

Floating people are a relatively new addition to the world of magic. But floating objects are part of a long tradition.

Theo Bamberg, known as Okito, (1875–1963) was greatly admired for his artistic presentations—the Floating Ball was a highlight that featured in many of his posters at the beginning of the 1900s. Norm Nielsen (b. 1934) levitates a violin that plays as it hovers. Harry Blackstone, Jr. (b. 1934) levitates a lightbulb that continues to glow as it sails above the audience.

WIDE-RANGING WIZARDRY

Most magicians like to perform all kinds of magic at all kinds of venues. But some magicians keep to one type of venue and do circus magic or restaurant magic or children's parties. Some keep to one type of trick—for Houdini, it was daring escapes. The variety of magic (and magicians) is endless.

▲ Leon Bosco (1874–1920) was a comedian who joined forces with two magicians called Le Roy and Talma. As this poster shows, Bosco kept to comedy by performing tricks that usually ended in disaster!

▶ The two stars of circus magic were Emil Kio (1894–1965) and later his son Igor (b. 1944). At the Moscow State Circus, they presented big, spectacular illusions—such as the magical transformation of a woman into a roaring lion. The woman was Emil's wife.

An all-rounder

Sherry Lukas used to be a magician's assistant and now has a full-evening show of her own—with everything from intricate sleight-of-hand tricks and dove productions to spectacular illusions.

A specialist

The Japanese magician Shimada (b. 1940) had a colorful act that mainly consisted of parasols appearing out of nowhere. (For the finale, he turned into a huge writhing dragon!)

Morocco the Talking Horse lived in the 1600s and belonged to a British showman named Banks. This beautiful white horse was so precious that it was shod with silver shoes.

Animal magic

Say "magic" and most people think of rabbits. In fact, magicians use all kinds of animals in their acts—everything from canaries to elephants.

In Egypt 4,500 years ago, a magician named Dedi performed several rather gruesome decapitation tricks with geese and other animals. Early this century, ducks and hens ran all over the stage and down the aisles in the comical Magical Farmyard of Le Roy, Talma, and Bosco. And in Las Vegas today, Siegfried and Roy have a show with shrinking tigers and vanishing leopards.

Morocco

Morocco the Talking Horse "spoke" by stomping his hoof to match the number of spots on a pair of rolled dice, or the number of coins in someone's pocket, or a person's age. In France, some people said this was witchcraft. Others said Morocco's owner used a secret sign to stop his horse stomping his hoof at the right number.

Munito the dog was said to have "a vast knowledge of geography, botany, and natural history."

The Learned Pig

The 1700s saw the rise of clever dogs and pigs that could pick out numbered cards to do simple addition, or letters of the alphabet to spell out replies to a question. William Frederick Pinchbeck's Learned Pig toured the United States and performed for President John Adams.

Beauty

One of the most famous dogs in the history of magic is Beauty. She was a gift from Harry Houdini to the German illusionist Lafayette (1872–1911). Beauty traveled everywhere with her new master. In the U.S. she had her own railcar. Her statue was on the hood of Lafayette's limo. In his London home, Beauty had her own bedroom, with specially designed furniture. Beauty and Lafayette are buried in the same grave in Edinburgh, Scotland.

The Vanishing Canary

Carl Hertz (1859–1924) used to make a cage and canary vanish at his fingertips. In 1921, British Members of Parliament were discussing a bill to protect performing animals. They asked Hertz to perform in the House of Commons—they had heard rumors that his trick killed a bird at every performance. Hertz showed them the trick and convinced them that no harm came to the bird.

▲ In Melbourne, Australia, in 1892, Carl Hertz advertised for 1,000 cats in return for one free ticket per cat. Young fans rounded up stray cats. Then Hertz's assistants tied signs for his show to the cats and set them loose. It worked—the show was a sellout.

The not-so-clever camel

Harry Blackstone, Sr. (1885–1965) once had a problem with a camel that wouldn't stand still. First the animal was placed in a striped tent. When the tent was dismantled the camel had vanished—but then it poked its head out from behind a false backdrop and gave the game away!

The Vanishing Camel

Comedy magic

Magic can make you not only gasp in surprise, but also roar with laughter. The comedy may come from the performer's odd appearance or from the clever patter (or talk). Or it may come from the situation (or story) created on stage.

Often a trick seems to go wrong, or the props are absurd. An ordinary magician changes a cane into a beautiful silk scarf—a comedian is more likely to change it into a string of sausages. Chinese linking rings link to everything in sight, tables fall apart and sprout human legs, bottles multiply beyond control, and mayhem rules the day.

But even as you giggle you still ask the question, "How do they do that?"

"Oops..."

The Human Hairpin
The British performer Carlton (1881–1942) exaggerated his gangling appearance with a fake crown and platform shoes. When he tried to vanish one of a pair of dice in a box, he clearly cheated by tipping it from one side of the box to the other. The audience ordered him to open all the box doors at once, whereupon the die really did vanish.

A famous fez
Britain's Tommy Cooper (1922–1984) was famous for wearing a silly fez and saying "Just like that!" as yet another trick fell flat. In fact he used a huge range of crazy outfits, corny jokes, and comic props.

"Just like that!"

Watch out!
In 1942 Laurel and Hardy appeared in the movie, *A-Haunting We Will Go*, with the great illusionist Dante. In it, they attempt to perform The Indian Rope Trick—whenever Hardy stops playing, the rope wobbles and Laurel tumbles to the floor.

Ballantine, the World's Greatest Magician?

Carl's classic

In the U.S., Carl Ballantine (b. 1917) botches the classic Cut and Restored Rope. He cuts a rope in half and drops it into a basket. The rope goes missing, so he virtually climbs into the basket to get it. Finally he holds up the rope—there's a gap. So how does that bottom half rise out of the basket?

The man who made ice famous

Something fishy

The character portrayed by the French comedy magician Mac Ronay (b. 1913) is a worrier, never sure why tricks don't work. For one trick he puts a fish into a bag. Later on he takes it out and finds it has been eaten!

Very often comedy magic relies upon involving an unsuspecting member of the public. The American comedy magician Frank Van Hoven (1886–1929) used to invite three young spectators on stage to hold a large block of ice, a candle, and a bowl of water. Van Hoven, however, couldn't make up his mind about who should hold what. While his three victims tried to keep up with his instructions, the ice slipped, the candle went out, and the bowl of water was spilled. Van Hoven shouted himself hoarse, and the act ended in chaos. He became known around the world as The Man Who Made Ice Famous.

Mike Caveney's Indian Rope Trick

A dove production

Like many magicians, The Great Tomsoni (b. 1934) produces doves from nowhere. But his doves often misbehave, covering his jacket in droppings! Unlike some comedy acts, Tomsoni's magic, although funny, does actually work.

Get out of that!

Escapologists specialize in escaping from chains, ropes, handcuffs, bank safes, packing crates, straitjackets—almost anything that seems totally secure.

Houdini is the most famous of all escapologists, but many other performers have also got out of impossible situations.

◄ **Australia's Les Levante (1892–1978) was frequently tied up, locked inside a packing crate, and thrown over the side of a ship. You or I would drown. But The Great Levante always escaped and swam up to the surface.**

It can take a long time for knots and padlocks to be checked or packing crates nailed down before the escape can even start. Nevertheless, a good escape act is nail-biting stuff—Houdini could keep an audience on the edge of their seats for well over an hour.

◄ Britain's most famous escape artist, Alan Alan (b. 1926), performed an escape while hanging upside down from a burning rope. He had just seconds to wriggle out of his straitjacket before the rope snapped and dropped him into a pride of roaring lions below.

► You've seen it in the movies, but in China the Australian magician Murray Carrington Walters (1901–1988) really was handcuffed and chained to a railway track minutes before an express was due. He had just managed to escape when the train thundered past.

An accident

Hans Moretti (b. 1928) was badly injured during a similar escape when the rope snapped and he fell to the ground. At least there were no lions this time.

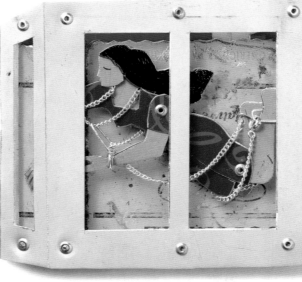

▲ Few escape artists have been women, but one exception is Princess Tenko. She performs a glamorous escape act during her magic shows in Japan.

Copy cat

A performer called Miss Undina featured a version of Houdini's Chinese Water Torture Cell in her act. Houdini was furious, and the show was canceled.

Don't do it!

You should never, never try any of these tricks yourself. Escapology (a word used by Houdini himself) can be very dangerous, even life-threatening. Of course the experts are well prepared after hours of practice and checks. But things can go wrong. Even Houdini, the greatest escapologist of all, got into difficulties. He broke three bones in his wrist performing a tricky escape in his movie *The Master Mystery*. And on two occasions he nearly suffocated—once inside a dead whale and once in a barrel of beer. So please don't even think about it!

Reading minds

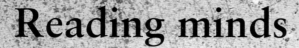 The mysterious act of mind-reading (or mentalism as it is known to magicians) has drawn people to the theater for over 200 years. In 1784, the Italian performer Pinetti blindfolded his wife on a London stage and asked her to identify objects brought up from the audience. She was able to identify snuffboxes and pocket watches, coins and hankies—anything!

Imprisoned

In 1949, Lesley Piddington was locked up in the Tower of London. She hadn't done anything wrong—she was about to name a book chosen by a member of a studio audience on the other side of the city. She succeeded.

Working solo

Some mentalists work solo, receiving thoughts from a member of the audience. America's most successful mentalist was Joseph Dunninger (1892–1975). He read the minds of the rich and famous, and made headlines by telling police where to find a stolen car. On radio and television he amazed millions by reading the minds of people who were outside the studio—in a submerged submarine, say, or in an aeroplane flying overhead.

Double acts

Some mentalists do a double act, like the Pinettis. In the 1925 Royal Variety Show, Miss Tree (get it?) presented a mind-reading act with her husband Leo. While she sat blindfolded at a piano on stage, King George V whispered the name of his favorite tune to Leo up in the royal box. Somehow, Miss Tree started to play that very same tune. It was *The Merry Widow Waltz.*

Audiences know that most magic acts rely on trickery. But with magicians who specialize in mindreading we are never quite sure—do they have genuine powers of telepathy or not? In 1949, Australian mentalists Lesley and Sydney Piddington told the press, "Judge for yourselves."

The ZANCIGS

MR & MRS JULIUS ZANCIG

"Two Minds with but One Single Thought"

The Danish mindreaders Julius Zancig (1857–1929) and his wife relied on a long and complex series of code words. There, now you know!

▶ The president of The Magic Circle, David Berglas (b. 1926), once found a letter hidden among the files in New York's Empire State Building, which is 102 stories high and contains an awful lot of files. So, how do you think he did it?

▼ As a publicity stunt, the Indian illusionist Sorcar (1913–1971) rode through busy Paris traffic on a bicycle while blindfolded. Do not try this yourself.

BECOMING A MAGICIAN

Where would the magician be without props? In every country in the world, there are dealers who sell magic tricks. Their shelves are packed with wooden boxes, metal tubes, feather flowers, and mysterious contraptions to tempt the visiting magician. For the magicians who cannot come to the shop, the dealer sends out a catalog.

Magic dealers also sell books and videos about magic, and give advice on how tricks should be performed. Many of them have secret "back rooms" where performers gather to discuss and practice magic.

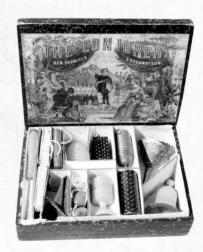

◄ **Many performers owe their start to a magic set containing tricks and instructions.**

Famous dealers

Robert-Houdin used to visit the shop of Père Roujol in Paris. This first opened in about 1820 and is probably the oldest dealership in the world. The oldest in Britain is Davenports of Charing Cross, London. It is still being run by the family that set it up in 1898. One of the world's largest dealers is Tannen's in New York, which was established in 1938.

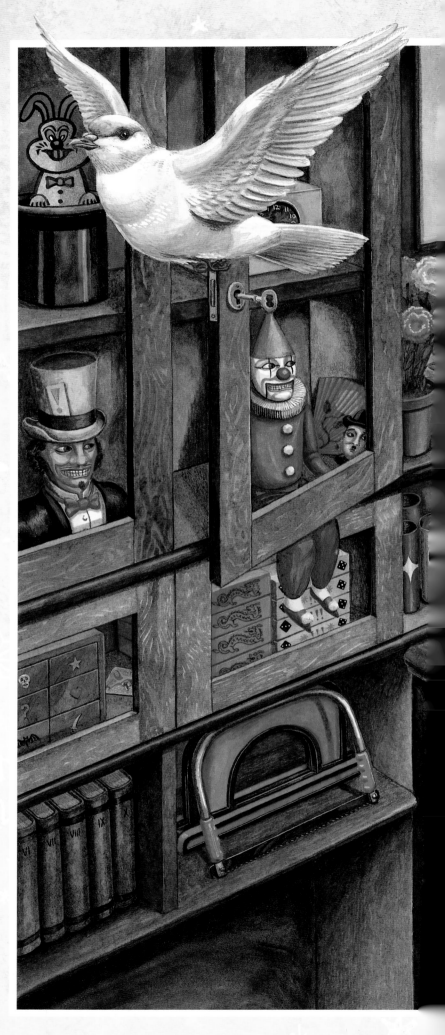

Eliaser 1760–1833

Dutch dynasty

The secrets of magic are passed down from one generation to the next, often in the same family. The most famous dynasty is the Bambergs. First there was Eliaser Bamberg, who claimed to be the son of a Dutch alchemist and a student of Pinetti. He had a wooden leg with a secret compartment and called himself The Crippled Devil. His son David Leendart and grandson Tobias both learned the trade. Next came David Tobias Bamberg who, like his father, was a conjurer at the Dutch royal court. David's son Theodore took the name Okito and performed as a Chinese magician all over the world. Okito's son, David Tobias Bamberg, was the last of the dynasty and performed as Fu Manchu.

David Leendart 1786–1869

Tobias 1812–1870

David Tobias 1843–1914

Okito 1875–1963

Learning legerdemain

Most magicians begin their studies with books. The first English book to explain how tricks are done was *The Discoverie of Witchcraft* (1584) by Reginald Scot. He wanted to prove that conjuring was not witchcraft. Since then thousands of books and videos have been published. To protect the secrets of the trade, they are sold only through official magic dealers.

▶ **Reginald Scot could not convince King James I of England that magic was harmless. The king ordered all copies of his book to be burned. So an original copy is now very rare indeed.**

Fu Manchu 1904–1974

The best way to learn magic is in a one-to-one teaching session with an established magician. There are schools that offer this kind of tuition. The most famous one is the Chavez School in the United States, founded in 1941—David Copperfield studied there.

Some magicians give private lessons. Although they carefully guard their secrets from the public, they are very generous with ideas and advice for young magicians.

In the magic circle

Most magicians are members of the magical societies and clubs that are found in every corner of the world.

Clubs help magicians to meet up and perform, watch, and learn new tricks. Go into any magic club and you will see billiard balls vanishing, cards rising, silks bursting into flames, and lively discussions about magicians and magic.

Most magic clubs also hold lectures by visiting magicians, exhibitions on the history of magic, and performances for the general public.

Magic in London

The Magic Circle was formed in 1905. Its London headquarters house the Centre for the Magic Arts with a theater, library, and museum open to the public. Magicians and amateurs alike are members of this famous society. The best are elected to the elite Inner Magic Circle.

▼ Every magic club has its own specially designed badge of membership. There are some famous examples here—how many do you recognize?

The Magic Castle

The Magic Castle in Hollywood, Los Angeles, looks like a fairytale palace. In fact it's the head-quarters of a club for magicians, and has a theater for performances by the top stars in the United States. The castle was built in 1909, taken over by the Larsen Brothers in 1962, and opened to magicians in 1963.

▲ The Magic Castle is the headquarters of the Academy of Magical Arts, which is dedicated to the advancement of the art of magic. Most of the major stars of magic have performed here.

Magicians also go to conventions where hundreds, sometimes thousands, gather to watch demonstrations and buy new tricks from the magic dealers who also attend. Then they go home and practice. That's really the secret of every great magician's success— practice, practice, and more practice.

Famous clubs

The first magic club on record was the Société Philomagique in Paris, France, established in 1820. The oldest still in existence is the Society of American Magicians (est. 1902).

The biggest is the International Brotherhood of Magicians (est. 1922). It has branches called "Rings" all over the world.

Joining a club

One of the best ways for a would-be magician to learn more is to join a magic club. Entry is normally by examination, so you'll need to learn some tricks first. Most clubs have a minimum joining age of 16 or 18, but many also have junior sections for younger magicians. Good luck!

An A–Z of the all-time greats

Amateurs

King Edward VII liked magic so much that he actually took lessons. His great-great-grandson, Prince Charles, is a member of The Magic Circle in London.

Also: engineer Isambard Kingdom Brunel; writers Charles Dickens and Lewis Carroll; W. S. Gilbert of comic-opera fame; film stars Charlie Chaplin, Will Rogers, Cary Grant, Orson Welles, and Barbara Stanwyck; talk show hosts Johnny Carson and Dick Cavett; boxer Muhammad Ali; General Norman Schwarzkopf; and you!

John Henry Anderson
(1814–1874)

Scots-born Anderson was one of the first to take magic from the streets and into theaters. The Wizard of the North advertised his name everywhere— from pats of butter and city sidewalks to the pyramids and Niagara Falls. Although he made several fortunes, Anderson died bankrupt.

The Bambergs
See page 50.

David Berglas (b. 1926)

The president of The Magic Circle specializes in mind reading and astonishing feats of memory—as well as a pickpocketing act! He has starred in TV series in Britain, Holland, Germany, and Sweden.

Harry Blackstone, Sr. (1885–1965)

Chicago-born Harry Boughton performed under several names before settling on Blackstone in 1918. By the end of the 1930s he was America's top illusionist. He stopped touring in the 1950s, but continued to appear on TV up to his retirement in 1959. Blackstone was the first magician to feature in a series of comic book adventures— a measure of his huge success.

Harry Blackstone, Jr. (b. 1934)

This TV star began by assisting his father during school and college vacations, eventually becoming a professional magician in 1954. His show includes several items made famous by his father—such as The Dancing Handkerchief and an amazing Floating Light Bulb.

Signor Antonio Blitz (1810–1877)

When he went on tour across the United States, Blitz claimed to be Moravian to add an air of mystery to his act. In fact he was British, short, and very funny. A favorite trick was The Bullet Catch, but he dropped this from his repertoire when volunteers from the audience put brass tacks and other lethal objects in the gun barrel. When Blitz died, several performers borrowed his name as their stage name, because he had been so popular.

Bartolomeo Bosco (1793–1863)

This Italian magician was a master of close-up magic. So great was his expertise with The Cups and Balls that they were engraved on his tombstone. Bosco loved to perform —not only in theaters but in taverns, markets, and even on buses during his travels.

Matthew Buchinger (1674–1740)

Known as The Little Man of Nuremburg, this amazing magician was born without hands or legs. In spite of these disabilities, he was a master of The Cups and Balls, as well as being a fine calligrapher and musician.

Lance Burton (b. 1960)

Inspired by Channing Pollock, Lance Burton became a professional magician in 1980. He is now one of the world's leading magicians and has his own show in Las Vegas.

Kuda Bux (c. 1905–1981)

Mindreader Kuda Bux originally came from Kashmir, India. He made his name first in Britain and then across the United States as The Man With X-ray Eyes—he could see through even the thickest blindfold.

Cardini (1895–1973)

Richard Valentine Pitchford was born in Wales but achieved world-wide fame as Cardini. With top hat and tails, and a monocle in one eye, he played the part of a tipsy man puzzled by the sudden appearance and disappearance of cards, billiard balls, and other objects. Magicians still regard his silent act as one of the best of its kind.

Carlton (1881–1942)

London-born Arthur Carlton Philps was called The Human Matchstick or The Human Hairpin because of his long, thin shape (exaggerated by makeup, a false balding dome, and platform shoes). This shape, plus a squeaky voice and wickedly clever conjuring, made Carlton a big comedy star in Britain, Europe, and the United States.

Charles Carter (1874–1936)

Carter performed his first show when he was just ten years old. Master Chas Carter, America's Youngest Prestidigitator, became Carter the Great and toured the world with lavish illusions (and some of the finest posters ever). He performed all the classics, from sleight of hand and levitation, to sawing a woman in two or turning a lion into Carter. During his seventh world tour he died of a heart attack in Bombay, India.

Chung Ling Soo (1861–1918)

William Ellsworth Robinson was born in New York City and worked as stage manager for Harry Kellar and Alexander Herrmann. Then he shaved his head and staged his Chinese act as Chung Ling Soo. With spectacular illusions and clever publicity (such as the use of interpreters at interviews), he won worldwide fame. His career was cut short when he was fatally wounded in a performance of his Bullet Catch at the Wood Green Empire, London.

David Copperfield (b. 1956)

David Kotkin became interested in magic after visiting a magic dealer to buy a ventriloquist's dummy. He staged his first show at 12, became the youngest person ever admitted to the Society of American Magicians, and by 16 was teaching magic at New York University. Still in his teens, he took the stage name David Copperfield and the lead role in a musical called *The Magic Man*. He is now the best-known magician in the world.

Paul Daniels (b. 1938)

Britain's leading magician got the magic bug after reading a book on the subject when he was 11. He gave his first performance a few years later and became a professional magician in 1969. Audiences liked his chatty style— within a year he was the top magician in Britain and has remained so to this day.

Dante (1883–1955)

Harry August Jansen emigrated from Denmark to the United States with his parents when he was six. He became an avid magician after seeing Alexander Herrmann. In 1922 he was hired by Howard Thurston, who gave him the stage name of Dante and sent him out on tour. In 1936 he opened at the Alhambra Theatre, London, with his own show, Sim Sala Bim—these three nonsense words from a Danish nursery rhyme were his trademark, spoken as he acknowledged applause. Posters boasted of 50 mysteries, and the show ended with Dante creating a cascade of fountains across the stage.

Dedi (c. 2500 B.C.)

Dedi's performance before King Khufu, the builder of the Great Pyramid at Giza, took place about 4,500 years ago. The Westcar Papyrus records that he mostly cut off the heads of birds and other animals and then made them whole again. Dedi's remarkable age (110) was attributed to a daily diet of 500 loaves of bread, a shoulder of beef and 100 jugs of beer.

David Devant (1868–1941)

Still regarded as one of Britain's greatest magicians, David Devant was born David Wighton. He performed at Egyptian Hall and then, in partnership with J. N. Maskelyne, at St. George's Hall, London. He became the first president of The Magic Circle in 1905. Devant was also a prolific writer, teacher, and inventor of magic. His most famous illusion is probably The Artist's Dream—a picture of a girl is magically transformed into life but then returns to being a picture.

Buatier de Kolta (1847–1903)

This Frenchman is unusual in the history of magic—not because he trained first to be a priest and then an artist, but because most of his tricks were his own inventions.

Many of de Kolta's inventions (such as The Flying Birdcage and The Vanishing Lady) are performed to this day. He always wore several pairs of pants, three pairs of stockings, three undershirts, and three coats, to avoid becoming ill while traveling—sadly, he died of Bright's Disease on tour in the U.S.

Ludwig Döbler (1801–1864)

Ludwig Leopold Döbler was a dazzling success. He was the first magician to have a street named after him—Döblergasse, in Vienna, Austria. Young men in Vienna copied his dress. His show opened with him lighting 200 candles with a single pistol shot (his rival, Philippe, lit 250 candles). After tours across Europe and performances for royalty, he retired to his country estate with a fortune.

Thomas Nelson Downs (1867–1938)

American Tommy Nelson Downs was renowned throughout the world as The King of Koins. He invented coin tricks and wrote books on the subject. One of his most famous tricks was producing dozens of coins from thin air—he called it The Miser's Dream, and it is still known by this name.

Joseph Dunninger (1892–1975)

Joseph Dunninger saw Kellar at the age of seven and was a professional magician by the age of 16. For 35 years he was The World's Greatest Mentalist. On highly paid TV and radio shows in the U.S., he solved impossible Brain Busters set by the audience or a guest celebrity. His one big mistake was to give away trade secrets in some monthly articles and be expelled by the National Conjurer's Association.

Isaac Fawkes (c. 1675–1731)

Fawkes was probably born in London, but little is known about him until 1720 when he had a booth at Bartholomew Fair. He did six shows a day, featuring an Egg Bag that contained much more than eggs, a musical clock and other clever automata. A ticket to his show cost one shilling. When he died, he had £50,000 and was the most famous magician in England.

Horace Goldin (1873–1939)

Goldin came to the U.S. from Poland and learned much of his craft from another Polish-born magician, Herbert Albini. His fast-paced style earned him the title of The Whirlwind Illusionist. In 1921 he struck gold with Sawing A Woman In Two—he soon had several companies touring with this illusion. Goldin's last performance was in 1939 at the Wood Green Empire, London, where Chung Ling Soo had died 21 years before.

Robert Harbin (1908–1978)

Harbin is regarded as one of the greatest modern magic inventors. He is best known for his Zig-Zag Girl illusion, but his fertile imagination led to hundreds of other tricks, too.

Born in South Africa, he made his debut at Maskelyne's in 1932 and remained a popular performer right up to his death.

Doug Henning (b. 1947)

Canadian Doug Henning took the magic world by storm when he starred in the Broadway musical *The Magic Show* in 1974. Dressed unlike any other magician in jeans and tie-dye T-shirts, he appeared in TV and stage shows but then retired from magic—he went on to run for public office.

Adelaide Herrmann (1853–1932)

Born of Belgian parents in London, Adelaide Scarcez was a dancer when she first met Alexander Herrmann. They married in 1875 and she became his principal female assistant. After his death, she toured with his nephew Leon Herrmann as the Herrmann the Great Company. From 1899 she had a successful solo act as The Queen of Magic.

Alexander Herrmann (1844–1896)

Born in Paris, France, Alexander Herrmann learned magic as an apprentice to his older brother Compars, who had been an assistant to his father, Samuel. As Herrmann the Great, Alexander became famous across Europe and the U.S. for heart-stopping levitations, decapitations, and bullet catches. He and Harry Kellar were bitter rivals, even pasting their own posters over the other's, but eventually they became friends. When Herrmann died, his wife Adelaide continued the show.

Carl Hertz (1859–1924)

Carl Hertz was born in San Francisco as Leib Morgenstern. His best-known act was The Vanishing Birdcage, which he performed for British MPs to prove the bird survived unharmed. This incident was typical of Hertz's flair for publicity.

Harry Houdini

See page 20.

Kalanag (1903–1963)

Kalanag was the stage name of Helmut Schreiber, and came from the character Kala Nag (Black Snake) in Rudyard Kipling's *Jungle Book*. Schreiber was originally a film producer in Germany. At the end of World War II, he toured Europe with the largest illusion show of the day. The highlight was the suspension and levitation of his wife, Gloria—he also vanished her, and the car she was sitting in!

Fred Kaps (1926–1980)

Dutchman Fred Kaps was regarded by many as the world's greatest magician. He performed magic with such charm and personality that everything he did seemed real. After his success on TV, audiences expected more charisma and technical perfection from others.

Harry Kellar (1849–1922)

This American illusionist began his career with the Davenport Brothers before forming his own illusion show and touring the world. In 1884 he opened his Egyptian Hall in Pennsylvania. He retired in 1908, naming Howard Thurston as his successor.

Emil Kio (1894–1965)

A star of the Moscow State Circus, Emil Kio performed a sensational cremation. A cloth cylinder was lowered over a girl in the middle of the ring and set alight. After the flames had burned the cloth to a cinder, a box was lowered from the ceiling—and out stepped the girl! When Kio died, his son Igor (b. 1944) took his place and the show went on.

Al Koran (1914–1972)

Born Eddie Doe in London, Al Koran became one of Britain's top magicians and specialized in mind reading on TV. When he died, his ashes were secretly scattered in the shops of magic dealers and on the stage of the London Palladium, Britain's most famous theater.

Lafayette (1872–1911)

When The Great Lafayette died in a fire at a theater in Edinburgh, Scotland, two bodies were identified as his—a look-alike had taken part in some of his quick-change illusions. For part of his show Lafayette turned into a popular Chinese conjurer, Ching Ling Foo. But in an illusion called The Lion's Bride, the girl in the cage was rescued only when the lion turned into Lafayette! Born Sigmund Neuberger in Munich, Germany, Lafayette became one of the most successful magicians in the world, and rather eccentric—he always traveled with two footmen, who had to salute him, and his dog Beauty, with whom he is buried.

BEAUTY

Servais Le Roy (1865–1953)

Belgian Servais Le Roy ran away to England as a boy and was adopted by a family there. He became interested in magic after watching a magician perform The Cups and Balls so badly it was obvious how the trick was done. In 1890 he married his assistant Talma (whom he also levitated and vanished in midair). From 1904 to 1930 they teamed up with Leon Bosco and toured the world. Le Roy had to retire in 1930, after being crippled by a car accident.

Les Levante (1892–1978)

Australia's most famous escapologist was born Leslie Cole. He produced his first full-evening show of magic when he was 20 and went on to tour the world as The Great Levante.

John Nevil Maskelyne (1839–1917)

Maskelyne became a magician after seeing a "spiritualistic" show in his home town of Cheltenham, England. He went to London and, after a season at St. James's Hall, he and his partner George Cooke went to Egyptian Hall and stayed for 30 years. From 1905 to 1915 he was in partnership with David Devant at St. George's Hall. As well as being a skillful performer and business man, Maskelyne was a brilliant inventor—his act included mechanical figures such as Psycho the card player, Zoe the artist, and Fanfare the trumpet player. After his death his sons, and later his grandsons, continued the family tradition.

Jeff McBride (b. 1959)

American Jeff McBride has a unique act that combines magic with mime, the martial arts, and Japanese Kabuki. He has performed all over the world, but mostly in the United States, Europe, and Japan.

Hans Moretti (b. 1928)

Polish-born Hans Moretti performs spectacular escapes and exciting illusions. He invites spectators to thrust swords into a box while he is inside. He escapes from a straitjacket while hanging from a burning rope. And he suspends his wife Helga on a paper tree.

Murray (1901–1988)

Murray Carrington Walters was an Australian illusionist who specialized in escapes—police in 42 countries failed to restrain him. He retired in 1954 to become a magic dealer in Blackpool, England.

Nicola (1880–1946)

William Mozart Nicol was born in Iowa. After assisting his father, Nicoli, he launched his own professional career as Nicola. In 1900 he visited the International Exposition in Paris and returned to the United States with several new tricks. In 1939 a world tour of his biggest show ever was cancelled when the ship carrying his props was sunk by a mine in Singapore. He carried on, performing small-scale magic for Allied troops in World War II.

David Nixon (1919–1978)

The top British magician of his time, David Nixon was best known for his long-running television show, *It's Magic.*

Penn and Teller

The American performers Penn Jillette (b. 1956) and R. Teller (b. 1949) stage a comedy act that has won them TV fame. They have been called The Bad Boys of Magic because they frequently tell the audience how the tricks are done.

Jacob Philadelphia (c. 1734–c. 1800)

Born Jacob Meyer, Philadelphia was the first American magician to perform in Europe. Frederick the Great banished him from Berlin, Germany, for revealing too many imperial secrets—so the magician made a spectacular exit through all four gates of the city at once.

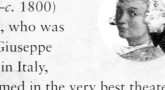

Philippe (1802–1878)

Born Jacques André Noël Talon in France, Philippe became interested in magic after seeing Anderson in Aberdeen, Scotland, where he was working as a pastry chef. Wearing a long pointed hat and flowing robes, he called his show *A Night in the Palace of Pekin.*

Pinetti (1750–c. 1800)

Pinetti, who was born Giuseppe Merci in Italy, performed in the very best theaters at a time when most magicians were still street performers. In Berlin, Germany, he had such a fine coach that the jealous king of Prussia banished him from the city. After two books by Henri Decremps exposed his methods (often incorrectly), Pinetti stopped performing and spent the rest of his life in Russia.

Channing Pollock (b. 1926)

American magician Channing Pollock won international success with his dove productions and clever card manipulations. Other magicians developed similar acts, but his immaculate style was hard to rival.

Richard Potter (c. 1783–1835)

Richard Potter was born in Massachusetts and was the first American magician to achieve fame in his own country. For over 20 years he toured the United States and Canada with his ventriloquism act and 100 "curious but mysterious experiments with cards, eggs, money, etc." He was buried at a site named after him, Potter's Place, in New Hampshire.

Richiardi, Jr. (1923–1985)

Richiardi was born Aldo Izquierdo in Peru. His father and grandfather had used the stage name Richiardi, so when Aldo began performing as in Argentina in 1943, he used the stage name Richiardi, Jr. He toured South America, North America, Europe, Asia, and Africa with an elaborate show that included Sawing Through A Woman (with "blood" spurting from the body) and The Broomstick Suspension.

Jean Eugene Robert-Houdin See page 14.

P. T. Selbit (1881–1938)

Londoner Percy Thomas Tibbles became a professional illusionist in 1900 and reversed his real name to get Selbit. He was a fantastic inventor of illusions. The best-known is Sawing Through A Woman, but there was also The Wrestling Cheese—spectators were invited to tip over or move a giant cheese that refused to budge!

Siegfried and Roy

The German illusionists Siegfried and Roy (Siegfried Fischbacker, b. 1939, and Roy Horn, b. 1944) met when Siegfried was performing on a cruise ship and Roy was a ship's steward. Roy had a pet cheetah and told Siegfried to use it in his act. They became partners—since 1967 they have performed all over the world, but mostly in Las Vegas, with a spectacular line-up of tigers, elephants, and even flamingos.

Slydini (1901–1991)

Slydini was born Quintini Marucci and learned magic from his father. As a teenager, he left Italy for Argentina and worked in vaudeville theaters until 1930. Then he moved to the United States. He became famous for close-up magic and his superb use of misdirection.

P. C. Sorcar (1913–1971)

Pratul Chandra Sorcar was the most famous Indian magician of all time. He built his sets, ran his publicity campaigns, and lived with his family all in a five-story building in Calcutta—in between touring the world with illusions such as his Sawing A Woman In Half. He died on tour in Japan, so his son Sorcar, Jr. took over the show.

Talma (1868–1944)

Born Mary Ann Ford in London, Talma married the magician Servais Le Roy in 1890. She later became a magician herself—The Queen of Coins had small hands, but she could palm 30 coins at once.

Howard Thurston (1869–1936)

Born in Ohio, Thurston had several jobs before deciding to study as a medical missionary—until he saw Herrmann the Great. He toured the vaudeville theaters with a card manipulation act. The high spot was when selected cards floated from the pack up to his waiting hand. After a successful tour of Europe, he developed one of the biggest shows of all time and was America's top act for 30 years.

Félicien Trewey (1848–1920)

This skillful French magician was renowned for his versatility. In addition to his "chapeaugraphy" (turning a simple piece of felt into 20 different hats) he could also juggle, sing, and do acrobatics.

Dai Vernon (1894–1992)

Known as The Professor because of his immense knowledge of conjuring, Dai Vernon was born David Verner in Canada. He devised countless close-up tricks and greatly influenced 20th-century magic. In 1963 he became Resident Magician at Hollywood's Magic Castle. People from all over the world flocked to learn from him.

Weber-aner

See page 8.

Finally, where would we be without...

Inventors The Austrian performer Johan Nepomuk Hofzinser (1806–1875) invented several tricks but when he died his wife, following his instructions, destroyed all his notes. Luckily one of his pupils continued to perform his tricks and these were eventually written down for the benefit of later magicians. (See Buatier de Kolta, who is one of the greatest magic inventors of all time.)

Teachers *The Tarbell Course in Magic* is the biggest available. It was created by Harlan Tarbell in 1927 and volumes continued to be published under the same name after his death. Tarbell (1890–1960) was also an excellent illustrator and inventor of magic.

Historians Through the ages, tales of magic have been handed down (and exaggerated with each retelling). The scribes of the Westcar Papyrus gave us the first records of magic performed as entertainment in Ancient Egypt. Milbourne Christopher and Edwin Dawes are recommended reading for anyone interested in the more recent history of magic.

Collectors John Mulholland (1898–1970) was the world's leading collector and authority on magic right up to his death. Now David Copperfield has established the International Museum and Library of the Conjuring Arts, a huge collection of posters, books, documents, costumes, and props.

Glossary

acquitment The secret transfer of a hidden object from one hand to the other.

ad lib An unscripted remark or action said or done on the spur of the moment.

amateur A magician who does magic as a hobby and not for a living.

angle proof A trick or sleight that can be viewed from any angle without the spectators seeing how it is done.

apparatus The visible equipment used in the performance of a trick.

assistant A magician's helper who forms part of the act.

audience participation The involvement of all or part of the audience in the performance of a trick.

automaton A mechanical model or figure that performs intricate movements and tasks.

betcha A challenge to the spectators in the form of a bet.

billet A folded slip of paper, usually with a word or number written on it, which the magician or mentalist has to identify.

book test A mindreading trick in which the performer divines or predicts a chosen word or a passage from a book.

box jumper A magician's assistant. So called because he or she spends a lot of time getting in and out of boxes or cabinets.

close-up magic Tricks that are designed to be performed with the audience at close quarters.

confederate A helper who appears to be an ordinary member of the audience but who is secretly in league with the performer.

cop To secretly get ahold of something that has been hidden.

cue A word or action that is used as a signal to another person backstage, or to someone already on stage, or to musicians.

dealer A person who supplies magicians with tricks, books, videos, and other items.

ditch To secretly dispose of something no longer required.

effect Any trick, but as it is seen by the audience.

emcee Abbreviation for Master of Ceremonies.

escapology The art of escaping from ropes, handcuffs, and other restraints.

ESP Stands for Extra Sensory Perception, the apparent ability to perform feats of mentalism.

exposure The disclosure of the secret method of how a trick is done—the big no-no in magic.

fake An object or piece of apparatus that appears to be genuine but isn't. Sometimes spelled feke.

fan To spread out a pack of playing cards so they form the shape of a fan.

fanning powder A powder applied to playing cards to make them slippery and easier to fan.

finale The finish to a trick or act—it is usually something more impressive than what has gone before, so that the performance ends on a high note.

FISM Stands for the Fèdèration Internationale des Sociétés Magiques (International Federation of Magical Societies, est. 1946) and also for the convention it holds every three years.

flash To allow, accidentally, the audience to see something that is supposed to be hidden.

flash paper Specially treated paper that produces a dramatic flash of flame when it is ignited.

flourish A visual display of dexterity or skill that is designed to impress rather than mystify.

fluence To put the audience under the magician's "influence", with a dramatic gesture and penetrating gaze. This usually takes place at the start of a mindreading or levitation act, to convince the audience of the magician's psychic powers.

force To appear to give a spectator a free choice but actually make them select what the magician wants.

foulard A large scarf or cloth cover.

gaff An object that appears ordinary but which has been specially altered for a trick.

get-out Any way of covering up the fact that a trick has gone wrong, without the audience being aware of the mistake.

gimmick A secret piece of equipment that enables the magician to perform a particular trick.

IBM Stands for The International Brotherhood of Magicians, which was founded in 1922 and is the world's largest magical society.

illusion A large-scale trick, usually involving people or animals.

impromptu A performance or trick done without any special preparation.

layman A nonmagician.

legerdemain A French word for sleight of hand, from *léger de main*, meaning light of hand.

levitation An illusion in which a person or object rises into the air with no apparent means of support.

load To secretly put an object or objects into position before revealing them. The word also applies to the objects that are loaded.

manipulator A stage magician whose act is accomplished mainly by sleight of hand.

master of ceremonies The person who introduces performers to the audience when a show consists of several acts.

mentalist A performer who specializes in magic of the mind.

mime The art of portraying actions or a character without using words. The same technique is also used by circus and theater performers.

misdirection The art of diverting a spectator's attention away from a secret action.

opener The first trick of an act.

out See get-out.

palm To hide an object in the hand.

patter The storyline, jokes, or other talking that accompanies the performance of a trick.

pellet A piece of thin paper bearing writing and rolled into a ball, used in mentalism.

penetration The effect of one solid object passing through another solid object.

piracy Stealing, copying, or selling tricks that belong to another performer—a crime that is frowned on by magicians everywhere.

pocket trick A close-up trick for which the items needed can be carried in the magician's pocket.

piracy

practice The repeated performance of a trick until it is second nature to the magician and can be done without giving any clues.

prestidigitation A French word for sleight of hand. It comes from the French word *preste*, meaning nimble, and the Latin word *digitus*, meaning finger.

production Making objects or people appear from thin air.

props Short for properties—the apparatus and other items that are used in a trick.

pull A method of vanishing an object by pulling it up a sleeve or inside a jacket. This gimmick is not used nearly as often as the public suspects.

rehearsal A practice-run of a complete act or show to make sure everything goes smoothly.

routine A sequence of actions that blend into a trick or a series of tricks.

running gag A joke or funny action that is repeated several times during a performance.

SAM Stands for The Society of American Magicians.

servante A hidden shelf at the back of a table or chair.

running gag

silk A colored square of fine material.

sleight of hand The manipulation of ordinary objects in the hands to create an apparently magical effect.

stack A secret arrangement of a few playing cards or a whole pack in a special order that is essential for the trick to work.

stage name The name used by a magician although it is not his or her real name—for example, Houdini was the stage name of Ehrich Weiss.

steal To secretly remove something from a place of concealment.

stooge See confederate.

sucker trick A trick that gives the audience the impression they know what the magician is up to before the magician proves them wrong.

suspension An illusion in which a person or object remains suspended in midair after some or all supports have been removed.

switch To exchange one item for another that appears to be identical, without the audience being aware that anything has changed.

table hopping Performing close-up magic at tables in a restaurant.

talk The sound made when a hidden object accidentally hits something in a performance and thus discloses its presence.

transformation The illusion of turning an object or person into something or someone else.

transposition The illusion of vanishing an object or person from one place and then producing them in another.

trap A secret trapdoor in the floor of the stage, or a hidden flap in a prop.

vanish To make an object or person disappear.

ventriloquism The art of speaking so that the voice seems to come from somewhere or something else.